Love and Lust

Love and Lust

Lorenzo Jackson

To order additional copies of this book, contact:
Xlibris Corporation
1-888-795-4274
www.Xlibris.com
Orders@Xlibris.com
86229

Contents

Passion's Definition

Walk in front of me,
leave my hands held on those hips,
and let the deep coldness of my words lay a trail of goose bumps
down your neck and back.
Catch my looking at you from a distance,
no I wanted you to look away cause your beauty should never be caught,
since my addiction for you makes me work for it.
How does it feel you ask? Baby girl imagine this: a conversation
separating each word with a kiss to sound like,
"What—is—passion?"
and nothing else would leave your lips after;
cause you probably know,
I'm fluent in French.
And I'm pretty sure you can translate.
Also my hands,
I know they are lost at first,
but at the end of the day they always seem to be laced with yours.
Oh, you can keep them cause at the end of the day they always seem
to trace your figure,
before I close my eyes to dream about you.
Almost forgot my eyes weren't green before but it seems the green
stitching up and down your jeans (which is green) and those blues
and yellows across your body,
which I guess after staring at them for so long you left me with a
beautiful blend of greens to make the emeralds you wear but you
haven't noticed yet.
One more thing,
my definition for passion,
if you can call it anything else,

it's the fingerprints I leave on your body,
the motion of the tongue as it smoothes over the taste buds,
it is the sound of my name when you say it,
it's the time when you have no energy to get up after making love so
they lay into their arms not caring about their close company and
sleep into your dreams.
Passion is the greatest thing since love,
even if they do know each other passionately.

Hallmark Poem

Loose me past your thought,
Pass ideas that are never caught
Don't stop after our good byes.
Turn green to match my eyes.
Glued more than lips and hands.
I'm with you, on your demand.
Savor our moments in every case.
Not too fast, enjoy the pace-
as if we slow danced to everyday.
We're pulled closer, never away.
Being young love was our plus
Also together, you, I, and us.
Beautiful and gorgeous is not enough
To try and describe you, is always tough
But each season, each day, new words
So give me time, nothing stays unheard.
I lose one thing that keeps you hold,
Our imprint of our love we mold.

Believe It

Someone has left your heart cut
taken you from love in a mansion to a hut
wired you up to think you were kept
believing every word you simply just leapt,
into a temporary commitment which you thought was long term,
slept into his feelings saying the foundation was firm
buttered and coated with a fake fantasy fried,
telling everyone who knew you, that you simply had died
and went to heaven on his looks and his abs
his words were chapters and you were puttin' in tabs
loving his compliments
when in real life those were only garnishment,
cause all he really wanted to do was move on …

Believe It (Part II)

So may I be the man to follow up those pains,
knowing all good and well there is still ice in your veins.
Figuratively I know I don't have a decent chance,
when every man can follow but these girls don't want romance,
saying that you don't want your heart broken twice in one year,
so your turning love into a phobia when it shouldn't be a fear.
But wait; now it seems I'm being compared to the last dudes,
when the last time I checked my feelings to you weren't rude.
So be as it is when I feel the world can pair us,
who can blame Romeo for trying, when Juliet isn't over Paris?

Infatuated Connections

I am for you,
as the dew wakes up with the grass to see the sunrise,
I will be there the next morning to look into your eyes;
as the trees dismiss the leaves to come back to them next year,
you can expect see my smile on your heart, even if you're not here;
as the moon shows your beauty to the sea just to love it's reflection,
my words are pretty much the same but with less projection,
the world has it's loves so don't leave a lover with rejections,
you may have a choice but remember our deep connections.

Life Comparison

does one ever want to be with two?
a question many cliché hearts suggest
but one that is touched when it's looking at you
remodeled from the growth into adolescence
seems like it was only yesterday
my eyes weren't forever fixed to your presence
a beautiful figure wrapped in nothing but ecstasy
skin softens with the days
as time wait 'till you're the only one next to me eventually,
one of these words will fall in your hands
confidentially,
my mind drifts to your dirty demands
(listen) does the man on the moon ever reach for the lady on the sun
'cause I am him
and I'm sellin' the moon to get to where you're from
for so long you have been the light in the distance
one day I'll swallow my heart
so you'll know of my existence:
I am that, five foot seven green eyed exclamation point at the front
of your sentence in Spanish sittin' upside down 'cause my passion
for you isn't normal, but here I am in your sentence holding on to
the very word that describes you best, "¡estravagante!" spelled just the
way it sounds, 'cause I don't mask your beauty but with my upside
down exclamation point yell it; so as you and your extravagance
lives on the sun, you know that your dangerously gorgeous UVs are
loved by the moon.

Last Words

Grace my presence or it won't be graced,
too dirty for words so it must be faced
Push off the ground cause we move the world
My heart stays shined cause our love stays pearled
Never satisfied since man wants perfection
you say you're not it, but you're it's closest reflection
My hopes are high like the clouds silver lining
The color seems dull, but you're the reason it's shining

So I sit at the edge of this bed
Every thought of you circles my head
Dreams of the night before stays fresh
But nothing compares to you in the flesh
We walk through the days with the weirdest pace
Since our calendar changes slow, life isn't our race
Special if anyone can see me as close
But you're not anyone, just my heart's only rose.

My Version of It

Am I destined for it?
When I sit back and contemplate plans for it
Cut holes in my chest so I can show it
Thinking of each passionate steps toward it
Am I a man leaping for it?
Or am I just another young naive reacher of it?

I call myself toe tapping to its songs
I tap a little off but my heart sees no wrongs
even when it hears the other singers holding deep feelings
I guess people hide the point, but there's no reason for concealing
from the world when it:
expressed me
described me
defined me
joyed me
failed me
youthed me
blessed me
made me,
till I have realized I am not only destined for it,
but I plan to live on it,
leaving one kiss on its forehead,
to let it know if I ever leave I'm always coming back for it.

You Love Me More?

You love me more?
I guess you forgot you said I love you to a poet

(see) I have dreams and aspirations and you're apart of them all
you're the sun in my city when the other one falls
I catch all the raindrops when you leave the clouds in tears
stand with you against life when it's pressing your years
Don't believe it? You might as well start asking my guys
'cause you're every word when a conversation would arise
I'm not the fastest to love or the slowest to want to make it
Yet when I'm with you I change speeds cause the feelings aren't
    debated
my pockets enjoy the good vibes you leave with your texting
pictures of you all across my phone, I guess my obsession needs
    some correcting
also check the wallet it lays empty, but it's not new
no need to work my paper unless it's working for you
I don't pimp, lie, and play anybody
I love, touch, and kiss on that only somebody
a new lover, who could dare be a cheat?
when in this world there is nothing as sweet

Chalked Up (free verse)

File us down as two coarse hearts
smoothed out with the rough concept of love.
It is almost impossible to find answers,
when the outside character places labels on our eyes.
Love at first sight with us is an understatement.
But I'm sure you dropped each statement like a bad conversation
Yet with these influenced thoughts of me
You ripped off shirt and pants to bare-
ME, just ME, the real ME, indescribable ...

Too undeserving of your heart,
'cause there aren't enough stars for you, in me.
But I tried and placed my handful of stars to your night sky.
To find myself poor and you not any richer, but-
"Diamonds to the eyes" you would tell me
to prove to me I am enough.
Who am I to argue without the power to gaze past those stars?
But even with no telescope I know there is so much more beauty,
just in your essence.

Why am I mad at you for not eating up my:
compliments, flatteries, poetry, and love sick words?
I guess love can be read with the body,
So I burn it all and take the advice, with no remorse
Enlightened to this thought, I swear you would make any poet save
    a tree.
I know what everyone thinks
"These feelings were too soon," but just like the dew on the grass
Without it, I live thirsty

Mine, but Gone

You offered love to me in hopes of a better year
I offered back, but your hands disappear
I kiss them gentle and bring them back
Let's connect? You are what I lack
You step back, you seem withdrawn
I keep forgetting you are mine, but gone.

I write my soul almost everyday
You say it's good, do you look away?
Your tears never fall too fast to catch
So I stay here, like a key to a latch
Knowing this when you start to yawn
I am your dream, as you're mine, but gone.

Moon over stars when we look up
Morning comes, I don't get a, "what's up?"
I want you even if I'm put down
I'm the same as before I fell to the ground
New days are different, but we stay on.
Even though it's sad, you're mine, but gone.

My Answer

Baby girl you must not be hearin' me right,
since it seems like you text the same questions every night
"how much do you care?
you saw me today how you like my hair?
what you like about me?
since you do poetry why don't you write about me?"
ok, so I answer the first three,
but that last one is personal (see),

My love, could write a dictionary with just the letters of your name,
and you ask for a poem?
I just might write you a novel!
I live to turn your figure into a painting just by using alliterations
of your amazing anatomical adjectives, tracing your curves with
just a pencil
making my hobby an art as I take the lead and sketch your beauty
with one hand while the other is stroking your ego.
These simple descriptions holding beauty's conviction making
seductive depictions of an ever growing off beat, heart-beat, with
pretty feet
my sweet honey, worth twice my money whose smile so bright that if
you threw it in the air the room gets sunny.
So dangerously desirable that you create sparks when I'm flammable,
un-crammable meaning that I can't take you, all in one night,
who has the right?
When Rome being less amazing as you was built in the light.

Never savored by taste alone,
ear sewn to your voice through the phone.
So gorgeous that I pedal 50 miles,
not my style but I'm addicted to your smile.
So poetically,
I'm genetically inclined to leave you symmetrically described,
but I leave you this one time,
loving this one line, that after this poem
all questions should be mine.
so sit relaxed knowing you hold a poetic heart
from the start,
I'm just saying I got your stats and these words are the chart.

My Unscuffed Letter

Dear shoes,
I know you've been recently scuffed
don't preach the blues
the situation was rough,
see there was this girl in some pretty pink Nikes
shoes were clean, face was right
and it was lookin' like she liked me
I offered my hand which she really didn't mind
she switched in front
so I can inspect the sneakers from behind,
her walk was flawless
the look of her was gorgeous
understand black and white shoes I couldn't just ignore this,
I feel your pain
but you gotta' watch your tongue
see the moment was insane
there was love and it was young,
she stopped walking
turned to me, to look into my eyes
we stood there talking,
please believe, I tried to stop it
the conversation took my head
yet I didn't urge to drop it
she asked, "what's on for tonight?"
and I said, "my shoes …"
didn't know she would like that answer so now we're walking in twos,

she put my arm across her shoulder
and laced my fingers tight
you understand I had to hold her
considering we were together tonight,
we glided the night streets
and the never ending sidewalks
before long I forgot I had feet
she stopped once more
turned to me again like déjà vu
getting closer than before,
she took that step that led me to this letter
I grabbed her hips
she took my lips
I should have known better.

Confused On Lust

Is it true you hold a poets heart?
If so where should I start?

I think slowly
Letting my heart beat fast.
Grabbing memories from the past
Love should know me

I smooth the paper with my pen
Let it speak in my direction
My feelings push toward our connection
So I stop writing for a moment to grin.

imagine her face as she reads my word
It leads my hope of makin' her smile
she finishes but it's thrown to the tile
Not pleased, cause I knew it was absurd

But determined I think a second time
maybe it will be great
So for it I make a plate
And serve it up with my lust for rhyme

I want to please but it's confusing
Give a present? that's a joke!
I keep forgetting that I'm broke
so I continue with less amusement

I hit the door to pick up words from the street
step to the park just to enjoy new life
yet pleasing you today will be my strife
But I love 'love,' let's just say it's sweet

Lace fingers when hands are cold
She is beautiful it is always said
Knowing that none of my words will hit straight to her head
Maybe it is too old

The thought of love in one place
One body you care for more than your own
yet you would want to match her every tone
And forget the thrill of the chase

Settle my days down
till one day I make your smile stay
get a hammock for us both, to lay-
back and enjoy your last frown

hold on, Imma' write this out
Call this my greatest thought
final poem cause it's the only thing I got
And I don't care if she will shout,

"This poem was beautiful from the beginnin'
the sweetest thing I ever bitten
call me smitten
Cause I loved everything that was written"

Expressed

Soft spoken lips say soft spoken words,
I say what I can, but it all goes unheard.
Keep each distant phrase at heart,
Till one day my letters won't fall apart.
Share with me the pencil that you own,
That love gave to you almost unknown.
It wrote a picture prettier than Monet
With every intention that I will stay.
Peacefully stroking the white of the page,
Placing but only one person to its stage

Laced Fingers

Hand caressed by hand, taking in deep breathes so my lungs can give to my heart the air that the butterflies take. Pacing my words to match my speeding pulse keeps my lips dancing alone. If only you understood how deep love canals into a man's soul to at least touch the core, but you've cradled it.

Hopeless is a man to consider the few words in his vocabulary great enough to describe love and their feelings for it, yet every day for me, is a heart's attempt

Love's Sentences

Never have I felt converted to speak to your soul but only to your beauty, since the beauty has read my whole dictionary compared to your soul who hears single words that pass through the hearts filter. Happy to break lips for the smile but also to press them together for a kiss. The sweetest honey is guarded by the bee, and stays in painful reach yet even to have that one drop comes ecstasy in itself. So lay into my arms, taking me as you want, being but one man, for everything.

The Cheek

I think Shakespeare has said it best to be a hand upon your cheek
I have based my plans on stealing your heart hopefully it doesn't
    sound too weak
I will walk to you nice and slow call your name so you see me coming,
walk up a little slower then consider when to start running
ten feet away I lose my step sliding on a leak,
catch myself on your hips but leave my signature on your cheek
yes, one kiss on your cheek should start an accidental romance,
maybe it's cliché but other methods would have no chance
yet after the slip there will be a question mark disaster,
you have a choice to take my love or leave the moment even faster?

Three of Me and Her

Kiss my cheek
And walk away
with my number written on your hand
Two deep breathes,
One for me not walking away from myself
Two for not looking back
Yet not facing her I stand
in one spot, never moving

You may be the person staring
Looking in amazement as I stand still
But I've been there
I have walked pass myself standing
Though I don't stare at me
I just go about my day
laughing at me for being stuck
Yet laughing at myself hurts more than somebody else.

Forget me, It's her
I walked away with her hips
Love is blind but there is new vision
Simply the missing link in my life
Truly three people, plus her,
She doesn't look back
I do,
so I walk with her, stand with myself, and laugh at being lost

Artist

I glance once, but breathe hard as if I had been running for her exquisiteness, two miles away she sits from my heart, no, she never stands cause to her beauty my legs couldn't even stand to it. Her eyes so beautiful do not pose to my existence, more fixed to the other direction as to be serious at the other entity. Still, to be that other person holding her eyes for this moment would be better than peace to Gandhi. Her hands, stay glued laying upon her legs life-less, but reveal her classy aire. She presents herself with just her hands, speaking not only her personality but her life: as she folds them she is dignified, at her sides she's distant; yet now, they hold cupped with a smile, leaving me lost to her lips, those lips, sweet lips, no man has enough paper to describe. Soft, firm, glistened, pleasant, calm, a perfect presentation on something so gorgeous. As if God put life's little joys into them, and being unselfish complimented the rest of the life-art with those rose petals. Seems too much to write when I have not glazed the magnificent unsung, lustfully, heart-skipping beauty that she is, but being in my profession I don't leave one pleasantry "undrawn."

Deterred Love

Fixed to lock eyes forever, and I can't seem to break the chain, not saying that I tried, but as it looks nowadays you take my right brain creativity and my heart, so I'm stuck trying to put my hopes with osmosis to words. Saying that if heavenly bodies were compared to yours, I'll be better off staying in the world or saying that if love was in an oyster, I would pearl a sculpture of you and melt it because it's still not as beautiful as the real thing. I call myself sleeping but here I am loving you with my eyes closed cause you stay in my thoughts constantly. Some people call it luck, some people call it lust, call it anything that would make you feel better, but having her in my arms now keeps me from writing a million love letters.

My Symphony to Love

my symphony to love
orchestrated from no instruments
just implements of compliments
beaded together to create my frame
of love's mysterious games listing all of her gorgeous names
yet I live to add on to that necklace

As I see it the world lives to fall for the dancers
sure my zodiac is different but she loved this cancer
that sits in a desk fingering the tempos for her feet
so she can turn to one sound while my lyrical painting grabs the beat
and we sync to a hypnotic blend of living
by living for music and at this moment giving
society that portrait depiction
showing how instead of conviction
we can mellow love on her steps and my descriptions.

Inspired to Inspire

Desert gives no life back to an already thirsty Earth
proving to us living, that our life's dry to our worth
calling us "dust in the wind" no value to ourselves
that's why we have our own people hurting themselves
some know what we face cause they live it too,
we all are different but yet our problems aren't new.
Simple living as we consider our days complex
Another problem, new obstacles, "just give me the next"
we are promised this life, since we were that twinkle in the eye.
you believe that you're the only one. there's no need to lie?
"trust no one cause everyone lies," ... don't exclude yourself.
"look at those people in the magazine!" ... leave it on the shelf
you cry for love, life, and so many seducing dreams
save those tears, cause even your existence gleams
give hope to someone even if you don't have it
give love to someone even if they don't grab it
enjoying the beauty with every last thing
brings out your beauty past everything
Spit out society's life and through it, live your own
this world is ours, just let it be known.

Colored

Artistic
Or Simplistic way she colors me new
Lost
with the Cost of discovering this blue
Must
or just Lust as I look for the means
Same
color Game yet never any greens
En-vy
Cant Be, the reason that I'm down
Dirt-poor
no more, can I reject the color brown
So soaked
Pro-voked, to question every droplet
Same song
One wrong, my rain isn't purple its violet
With hope
I scope the world for this missing head
Too bad
Not mad, though my heart bleeds for red
Soft-me
Not-me though I compose myself to you
Seems like
I dis-like the same unloving blue.

Cheater

so you think I'm lookin' around when I have you in my arms
wrong guy 'cause you're the only girl who knows these boyish charms,
push me off like any other girl who says men all the same,
tell me, why you pullin' that card when you know the other game,
c'mon, I know you like you know me,
but lately you've been actin' like the same person ain't me
sure I can understand that you've been busy lately,
but if I'm free all the time; pretty sure your phone could take me
can't talk either? maybe if we were close I'd get some answers,
but right now I'm feeling like a low-paid back up dancer,
part of the show but no spotlight is getting' kinda' old,
I'm done talkin' 'cause your shoulder is gettin' very cold.

Say Diddo To Love

silhouette the fine tuned instrument I love to hear draw strings and
    I will draw a tint so beautiful that other shadows, including the
    one of the stars will fall to compare to you
a view that if placed on the ocean the sunset will not have room to
    replace you,
a touch so gentle feathers will ask for your secret
I listen to your voice and fall victim to a genuine love,
indescribable to Cyrano and unwritable to Shakespeare,
with a passion so deep and fiery that scientist have compared it to
    the center of the World
sweet, sweet to your lips is like calling a hurricane a breeze
never close, but even more amazing than it sounds
you have grasped all tastes buds with a kiss, just one kiss
a chef has never made a flavor so unique and amazing
so let's just say you are the perfect ingredient.
you stole my heart, what else can I say?
so I throw a rhyme in
about how you are the fantasy of the day
so undone to your looks and the way you speak
I will put handcuffs on my neck to your heart so everyday I'm
    whispering
love notes, sonnets, essays, paragraphs, sentences, definitions, refrains,
    songs, pentameters, couplets, haikus, limericks, etc etc
till "I love you" with MY cursive is chiseled so deep into the wood of
    your heart,

with the knife of my words that it will stain the very soul of your love
and leak to your mind so every now and then you'll be thinkin''bout my
deep phrases, constant compliments, long stares, shaky hands, slow
walk, lazy love stories, lame jokes, poetic attempts, long phone
talks, good morning texts, good night texts,
constant fear of losing you, urges to hold you, mold you, fold you,
lusting for a cold you, so I can give you my jacket that's warm
enough to make you sweat when it's cold
So make me a constant fantasy, cloning a lust for you that I've been
sleeping with for far too long.

Love's Theme

this is love's theme
deep breathes so we takin' in steam
peaches and cream
'cause we're livin' the sweetest wet dream

call it a personal magic
too good for video so we flashed it
don't trash it
cause any word less than beautiful would be tragic
mind blown
so I'm takin' Beyonce's video phone
with a new tone
stretching this moment like the o-zone
never done
savoring this moon, like a slow sun
we don't run
as we lay on this punch line with a good pun

cause it love's theme
deep breathes so we takin' in steam
peaches and cream
'cause we're livin' the sweetest wet dream

it's a pity
to wonder they made you so pretty
sounds so gritty
but here I wear your love like the name of the city

I could say never
but my heart is weak to this endeavor
she says she's clever
yet here we are, smitten together
so here we stand
sitting on the other's command
I post my hand
lips lock takin' every demand

so it's love's theme
deep breathes so we takin' in steam
peaches and cream
'cause we're livin' the sweetest wet dream

then I stopped …
I rolled my tongue till her hips dropped
her body un-topped
puttin' her up, so her back is propped
against this wall
she's waiting, hoping that no one calls
no sounds all
so today my heart is taking the fall-
for this passion
she seems to love all of my actions
the best reaction
is when the rhythm is matchin'

tellin' me its love's theme
deep breathes so we takin' in steam
peaches and cream
'cause we're livin' the sweetest wet dream

she whispers to me
"what do you want this moment to be?"
she leaves the key
so I tell her, leave your doubts with me.
I love her smile
as I trace the shape of the Nile
we're gone for miles
cause countin' time isn't my style
takin' my air
I lookin' into her proving I'm there
do I care?
I could tell you, but love didn't let me hear-

when it's simply love's theme
deep breathes so we takin' in steam
peaches and cream
'cause we're livin' the sweetest wet dream

I'm gonna' save my words
'cause everything that's been said has been heard
she cut me in thirds
but we stay high lovin' like a couple of birds
she holds me right
So undeserved that I question my sight
love was the fight
breathing heavy I guess we can call it a night.

Truthfully

Truthfully writing you the love of the day,
When there is so much to write I can't find what to say
Truthfully holding you I'm sure you have your doubts
Maybe the most quiet but there is temptation to shout
Understand MY temptations, as they live to lay with yours
Pain of your doubts leaves my fingers with sores
Because I'll write down my pains instead of say it
Make music with the sheets and start to play it
Find myself lusting too hard, for you, so I pray it-
Won't lead myself into becoming obsessed
She's my significant lover as she sleeps on my chest
My significant other when we're out at our best
PDA may be how the world might see it
But truth be told, if I say I love you, I mean it.

Our Potential

Simply let your feelings unlock
Since I want to sleep on them
In deep thought like "the thinker"
Sipping and enjoying all the lusts on your mind
I'm an addicted drinker
Taking it to the heart not the head
Call it seducing
Let's just say it's those dirty whispers
That's producing-
These, "get your mind out the gutter" phrases
Which usually keep you laughin'
Don't be too serious
When you're with me it'll never happen

Life so beautiful
Always pressing her essence
Life tried to leave its message
When she's with me, we void his presence
I'm always counting simple moments
That composed our complex connections
Walking lost through the night
As we leave our everyday with the directions
We are not the other lovers
Caught in the real
Sharing lips, hands, and hearts
Living on what love can reveal

Perfect Poem

my perfect poem is written for her to her and next to her, she was there as I held my pencil to write it, she was there to scratch my head when I ran out of rhymes, she was my acronym for every synonym to every metaphor, sure I can call to ask for help but who dare make the perfect poem without being next to perfect inspiration. Not me, cause you couldnt make it perfect unless you could feel the skip of her heartbeat writing in each adjective that described her; you couldnt make it perfect unless she giggled after every ironic, iconic, moronic, statement that you happened to slip in there when you were thinking about how she makes you laugh. It couldn't be the perfect poem unless she rised with your climaxes and fell to your poems conclusion, pressing your pulse as you write, conforming each gesture to her beautiful cursive to my unreadable print and making a blend of handwriting that everyone can read, relate, and recollect on. I have never met the perfect poet to write this perfect poem, but in the face of inspired perfection, together we have wrote what writers need to write and poetically defined a poem that every poet has poetically attempted cause in everyone's lifetime everyone deserves to have their inspiration when they write their perfect poem.

I Want to Live in Your Love

I want to live in your love
Holding on to my own beautiful fire
If you were to die in my love
Could I keep the desires?

I want to live in your love
As my hands quake to your touch
Trying to keep my control
When the love seems too much

I want to live in your love
When your voice melts the phone
Softens my final days
As I'm reminiscing alone

I want to live in your love
When I decide to be resistant
Holding back every memory
Knowing my heart is persistent

I want to live in your love
I want the life in your smile
I want that innocent love
Which walks together for miles

I want to live in your love
Remember in my dreams you are kept
Anticipating the casket
Dying for love while I slept

Whispers

Silence is silver when hearing your voice is gold,
Guesses can be made but are you really sold?
I'm bought! Without you getting the receipt …
My heart is always free, so the deals are always sweet.
Trust me and our butterflies; with others I have tried.
Don't believe me? Try me, because you even have my pride.
Since life offers 3 positives: hopes, dreams, and aspirations.
You gave me it all back with love, joy, and inspirations.
Mind is set, because I still feel for you now …
I'm unexplainably addicted, so don't ask me how.

Conversation

Excuse me miss
(Ok) I figured you would say I'm excused
You have that "step back" attitude
And I'm highly amused
I'm lookin to drop my number
So you could slip me a name
(so) you're gonna' ignore me
You know I can play it the same
But being this close
I feel your worth my time
Finest ten I've ever seen
Can you spare me a dime?
Yet being so beautiful
Can you live to hear it again?
Let me hold your eyes for a second
Just to give you a lens
Its my visual adjustment
Into a future with me
With nothing but love
And handful of poetry
Written with my fingers
Across the soft of your skin
With someone so seductive
Who needs paper and pen.

I'm a romantic you see
Planning to spit you a rose
Unlocking a beautiful essence
Hoping your heart can unclose

When your joy in your life
At most is a smirk
I'm a gentleman to know
When the other men don't work

I know, I know
I sound like the other thirsty guys
Spitting my game
While you're feastin my eyes
Stealing my heart
Addictively I'm longing to lust
Soaked in your essence
Holding your attention is a must
C'mon, zip up your jacket
Lets take a step out to talk
No not a creeper either
I just want this conversation to walk
(Oh) I understand
This advancement doesn't seem right
I'm a one language lover
Hoping you would grace me tonight

I'm a romantic you see
Planning to spit you a rose
Unlocking a beautiful essence
Hoping your heart can unclose
When your joy in your life
At most is a smirk
I'm a gentleman to know
When the other men don't work

So how does that sound?
A trade of words for steps
Getting to know each other better
Feeling on your soulful depths
Catching defining thoughts
That your heart can incline
Scratching the minds very surface
Can lead to a lovely define
Maybe, I'm rushing myself
'cause I'm sure you do have a phone
All I ask for is seven digits
To love your voice when your alone
Fixing your pains with every word
Call it a miracle voice
It can change how you love
Just please make me your choice

Untitled Dedication

Simply put, I am a smitten writer, thirsty for your love, I am never satisfied with just a good word, so I take my lighter, and begin to put flame to a lost thought.

Well, it wasn't lost when it was sketched, 'cause in my mind it was YOU, the very portrait of my heart, defined in the anatomy of my lust, you can trust, as I collect these words, so my pencil will turn to dust, due to the fact you're in my dictionary of two to three thousand pages, and If I plan to read it all, my tongue will be running for ages. Babe, you struck a nerve, with my lovely four letter word, and with these perfect details I will describe your every curve.

Always Different

These simple frustrations,
Turn into unattractive conversations
Putting our heads together knowing we end up bumping heads,
Wanting to leave but without my heart my body is dead
So I push to love you more knowing you love me less
I must confess,
That I'm in love with the other you,
But as of lately she comes only when the moon is new
True feelings make me feel something is wrong,
Make up, cause I'll give up
And just make the blame mine
You were wrong too but to keep you is fine.

Made in the USA
Lexington, KY
03 December 2010